AF338278

The Bronze Serpent

The Bronze Serpent

Liturgical Poems 1975–2014

BY
Edward Lense

EDITED BY
Deborah Fleming

ILLUSTRATIONS BY
Paul-Henri Bourguignon

RESOURCE *Publications* · Eugene, Oregon

Contents

II. Put Your Hand on Compost

III. Via Crucis: The Way of the Cross

List of Illustrations by Paul-Henri Bourguignon

Acknowledgements

Journals
Lost and Found Times: "Wrath"

Collections
Via Crucis: The Way of the Cross, a Human Pilgrimage:
poems in *Via Crucis*

Editor's Introduction

Edward Lense was a well-known poet and accomplished photographer in the Columbus, Ohio, arts community from the 1970s until his death in 2014. Having earned his Bachelor of Arts from New York University in 1969 and Doctor of Philosophy from Ohio State University in 1975, he worked as professor of English at Columbus College of Art and Design from 1976 to 2007 and served as advisor to the college's annual student magazine *Botticelli* (1976–2000). A long-time member of St. Stephen's Episcopal Church, he also served as deacon at St. Cyprian's Reformed Catholic Church in Columbus. His frequent readings were well-attended, he was a three-time Ohio Arts Council Award winner in poetry and criticism, and he reviewed books for *Ohioana Quarterly*. Although best-known as a poet, he also wrote three novels, short stories, a textbook on writing poetry, a libretto, meditations, and homilies. He translated poetry from Anglo-Saxon and collaborated with visual artists. His published scholarship and criticism include work on W. B. Yeats, James Wright, Robert Bly, Theodore Roethke, O. Henry, J. R. R. Tolkien, Len Deighton, and Thomas Pynchon. A talented chess player, he once drew with Grandmaster Bobby Fischer in a simultaneous exhibition. In later years he worked with the Columbus Literacy Council, teaching English as a Second Language to refugees and immigrants from Somalia.

Deeply interested in theology but never satisfied with the commonplaces of faith, Edward wrote liturgical poems that delve into the meaning of belief. Both free verse and formalist in style, they borrow imagery and narrative from biblical sources while revealing their implication for modern times. The verses in the first section, "Liturgical Poems," are mostly based on biblical passages.

Many are dramatic monologues spoken by characters from Bible stories and Christian tradition such as the Young Man in Gethsemane, Salome, the Pharisees discussing the man born blind, the shepherds and wise men at the birth of Jesus, the boy whose loaves and fishes fed thousands, Lazarus, disciples on the road to Emmaus, Thomas, Jonah, and St. Stephen; the lesson we learn from them, however, is not an easy principle of acceptance but the transforming epiphany of doubt become revelation after searching. These poems are set in the tradition of religious literature: "The Easy Yoke" contains echoes of Milton's humility; "The Road to Emmaus" of George Herbert's fulfillment of faith after disillusion; "Lazarus" of Donne's certainty of resurrection; "The Three Wise Men" of T. S. Eliot's mystical and mystified travelers; "Salome" of W. B. Yeats's spiritual dancers. I have chosen "The Bronze Serpent" as the title poem because the central image—the bronze serpent created by Moses which saves the Hebrew people from the deadly bite of vipers—prefigures the Christian story and because other images in the poem appear throughout the collection: transformative fire, living water, spiritual cleansing, sight become vision, certainty of salvation from "water that will flow/ from a broken body/ raised into the sky/ to guide us home to God."

The section titled "Put Your Hand on Compost" brings to life the meaning of the Seven Deadly Sins while avoiding sermonizing. The final section, "Via Crucis: The Way of the Cross" employs the stations of the cross to bring awareness of the human journey from experience to transcendence.

Most of the poems collected here were unpublished in Edward's lifetime other than those in "Via Crucis" which were printed in a chapbook (titled *Via Crucis: The Way of the Cross, A Human Pilgrimage*) to accompany the drawings of long-time Columbus resident and artist Paul-Henri Bourguignon (1906–1988).

For their immense help, thanks go to Lisa Iacobellis and Rebecca Jewett of The Ohio State University Library Special Collections and to Edward's long-time friends John M. Bennett and Catherine Mehrl Bennett of Luna Bisonte Prods.

I. Liturgical Poems

The Young Man in Gethsemane

> And a young man followed him, with nothing but a linen
> cloth about his body; and seized him, but he left the linen
> cloth and ran away naked.—Mark 14: 51-52

Who was he, this anonymous young man
for whom the sacred drama, unresolved, paused
just as Christ took his first steps toward the cross?

Whoever he was, he was not a Roman,
not a poor cripple waiting to be cured,
not a disciple who just lost his nerve;
whoever he was, his identity
nothing but rags clutched in the soldiers' hands
and shouts and confusion left in the dark,
he broke away, vanished from history.

Who was he then but the one who shrank from
Judas' kiss, the executioner's kiss,
turned toward the live dark, long life, turned and ran,
the air against him heavy with flowers,
naked, warm and free? Whoever he was,
he was only a man, one of us, not
part of the story.

The Dream of the Rood

Translated from Anglo-Saxon

Listen! I will describe   the best of dreams,
what I witnessed in   the watches of the night,
in the dark silence   where I lay asleep.
In the middle of the night   a miraculous tree
rose above me, lifted   high, wrapped with light,
crossed beams of light.   That shining beacon
glittered with gold;   great hosts of angels
shone with the beauty   of their birth in heaven.
I saw and wondered,   but I felt the wound,
the stain, of sin;   the splendor of that tree,
its gold, its diadem of jewels,   did not disguise
its pain, its suffer-   ing, its sorrow:
its right side bled, its wood   was soaked with blood.
Yet as I mourned in the dark,   dimmed light grew strong;
I saw the shining gold   glow clean again.
After a long time I heard a   low voice, weeping, say

"I remember how I lived   in a forest long ago,
how I was hewn down,   hauled off my roots,
made into a cross   and carried up a hill.
The ruler of all mankind   hurried to climb to me,
to use me as his gallows   tree against my will.
I did not dare,   against the Lord's desire,
bend or break,   or dare strike
and slay his slayers,   but stood fast.

They stripped and mocked   the man who was almighty God;
resolute, he strode   to where I stood,
brave against many men   to redeem mankind.
I trembled, but he held me;   I had to hold him up,
I dared not fall or bow to him.   I stood fast.
As the Cross I was raised up;   I raised up Christ,
Heaven's Lord, and dared   not lower him.
They drove in bloody nails and   made deep wounds in me.
I was stained with the blood   that flowed from mankind's side
as he gave up his ghost: I carried God
stretched out, his body   dead. Darkness
overwhelmed the earth.   The whole world wept,
mourned the King's death.   Christ was on the Cross.
His disciples came in the dark   and took his body down,
took down almighty God,   and laid him on the ground.
They left me standing, wounded,   soaked with his blood.
They gathered, a weary group,   where he lay on the ground;
he who had vanquished death   lay weary after victory.
The body of heaven's   King grew cold.
Mourning, they bore the body   away, bitter in triumph.
I was hewn down,   I too died on that hill,
that was my fate.   But I was the Lord's friend,
and he was my beloved;   I did not betray his trust.
God suffered on me to save   mankind from sin,
And now I am health and healing   to all who honor him:
I, cut down, tormented,   am the tree of eternal life."

Wind

> Are not two sparrows sold for a penny? And not one of
> them will fall to the ground without your Father's will.—
> Matthew 10:29

The sparrow's scythe-shaped wings
lash tip to tip, quick arcs
flurry to hold it still
head into the cold wind

my car noses smoothly
under the wind and stops
under the driving flight
held suspended, dead still
just out of reach, the wings
holding on to nothing
until the heart stops, wings
stiffen, it is swept back
or the wind drops, it feels
a lee and the wings grip
and thrust it safely home.

God watches from the wind,
God is the wind, the hand
that holds it, balances.
Because I am not God
I drive on.

The Tower of Babel

Blocks of stone the builders left behind, scoured
to sand by desert winds, drift into signs
drawn by the winds. They mean nothing. Words
said where the tower once stood mean nothing:
breaths we fill with shared
lives, breaths we send out
to meld our solitudes, silenced. Snakes mock
our waggling tongues, writing in cursive loops
meaningless words in the sands of Iraq.
This one place, in a world of many names, has none.
Those who enter it cannot know
truth from lies, their tongues confused;
only the flames of Pentecost can burn away its shadows.
Spirit of truth and life, save us from the death
of lies, fill our living words with your breath.

Shepherds

Luke 2:8–20

The angels almost came too late for us.
Night was just empty night for us,
stars just stars, sheep
mouths on bodies clumped along the hills
like low clouds, digesting in their sleep.
But all that night we basked in the fire of stars
and every word we spoke we sang, as though
music in our voices echoed music faraway, far above.
Our hearts, scarred over
with slights and hurts and grievances,
healed even before we left for Bethlehem.
It was not, after all, too late for us:
though we no longer hear the angels sing,
nights will never be empty again.

St. Stephen

Faces set, eyes chips of flint
they close on him like jackals
at the kill. They stayed at bay
longer than I expected,
Pharisees and Sadducees too slow to catch the swift run
of his thought, foot-tangled in
arguments as subtle as
his master Jesus; baffled,
they picked up stones to make their
argument and piled their clothes
at my feet, freeing their arms
the better to heave heavy
rocks jagged like their faces.
I shut my eyes and ears, turned
away as he turned to me
his smashed face, in it the face
I could not yet quite see.

Palms

In the first shoots
long before the leaves grow
broad enough to muffle a donkey's hooves
there are already
fire and ash,
in the green spears on wall
stuck behind picture frames
rustles
too slow to hear
as green withers into brown,
moist to crisp
ready to burn.
As ash after fire
enriches soil
its grit on flesh
makes us whole:
by the end of spring
new shoots will grow again.

Caedmon's Hymn

Translated from Anglo-Saxon

Caedmon, "slow" and shy,   swept out the stables
every evening, every morning   milked the monastery's cows.
He was always quiet, and took   no comfort in human company
but he was pious, perfectly   harmless, and stayed in his place.
One night, when table talk   turned to singing
old lays of heroes, long before   his turn he left
the hall and bedded   in the beasts' warm breaths
where Jesus lay on his first night.   Now nothing
but silence, and the spirit   speaking in a dream,
"Caedmon, sing for me."   "My voice is cramped, I cannot sing."
"Sing for me. Sing   the making of my world."
Then the simple herdsman   sang the song we hear in all our
     hearts:
Praise him who holds   Heaven's throne,
protects with his power   holy purpose
in all his works   and wonderful ways,
everlasting Lord   who gave life to the world.
He made by his might   for the children of men
the highest heavens   as a roof for our home
in Middle Earth: our Maker, our Master,
everlasting Lord   in whom we live,
our Giver, our Guardian,   almighty God.

Flames

Hebrews 12:18-19, 22-29

They hover over Bunsen burners, waver
mirrored in glass and steel, diminishing
down long tables into sparks
in chill white light but still
translucent orange, yellow, blue;
above each tip, invisible
as breath, the fire
at its most intense makes all it touches
change.

Salome

Before I could walk I knew how to dance,
Live in the swing and shiver of my flesh,
Stilled inside, trapped and dying in a trance.

I woke to whining music in a stance
Of lolling pleasure, neck and belly stretched;
Before I could walk I knew how to dance,

Knew how to disrupt any man's balance
Of mind and body, leave him weak and flushed,
Stilled inside, trapped and dying in a trance;

So when the king was stirred I took my chance
And smiled at his promise in the sudden hush;
Before I could walk I knew how to dance

Simulacra of passion, cruel romance,
Eyes hard with lust, bodies aroused, enmeshed,
Stilled inside, trapped and dying in a trance,

Shivering at what we saw on a soldier's lance:
Dead eyes pitying us all, the pitiless.
Before I could walk I knew how to dance
Stilled inside, trapped and dying in a trance.

Waking

I Samuel 3:2-18

After walking for so long I get out of bed,
the sheets behind me a landscape of dreams,
topography of failed sleep.
Wind slaps at the windows with open palms,
leaf shadows shift in white bars
cut out by streetlights bright as full moons
that light the corridors where I pace
busy as I was all day in a flurry of scuffs on bare floors
until in mid-step night without wind, without sky, only
a mind waking to finally ask the dark "Where am I?"
almost ready for the answer, almost
ready to listen to the quiet voice that will not let me sleep.

The Easy Yoke

The yoke settles on our shoulders, light
as feathers, but not wings. We fumbled
our burdens heads down, backs bent, far from flight,
under our own weight staggered and stumbled,
but the yoke that binds us now will not let us fall,
wings after all.

The Parable of the Thorns

Ripsaw edges of leaves, thorns
cut off light and air,
taproots desiccate the soil.
Our growth in these thickets is slow,
roots and stems tangled in theirs,
our slightness their strength.
But we endure:
we know the harvesters will
carry us safely to the threshing floor
while the thorns wither under crowns of fire.

The Three Wise Men

Every night when the sun set
we had come a day closer
to that strange new star we had followed all our lives,
it seemed, past ancient ruins, through wastes
of shattered rocks, sand mountains
shifting like uneasy dreams;
every night when the sun set
rocks, battlements, and sand,
even the dust kicked up by our feet,
glowed for a moment
pure burning gold
and, when days lengthened every spring
of the journey, when we looked up to the star
still leading us, soft night winds
brought the scent of cedars, flowers
and flowering trees new to us,
sweet as frankincense
and when we finally reached the place
beneath the star we found no palace,
as we expected, but a hut in a dreary
mud-brick village where the baby
lay in the stink of a stable
and the cloth that swathed him cleansed the air
as we, kneeling at the end of our journey,
were cleansed
with pungent myrrh. We could give him nothing
but what he had given us.

A Man Speaking with Authority

Heads hanging from bent necks,
eyes blank
behind shut lids, faces
transparent like mosquitoes
reddened by drops of blood, thoughts
he owes me money but still won't
speak to me, I saw the way he looked
at my wife, how soon will this be over?
humming insubstantial as insects' wings
and the acrid smoke of blood.
Then a man stood up, opaque,
unknowable, eyes dark fires
and I
crying aloud, not from pain
but surprise that empty men
are full again, and the man most
human knows me, knows everything I have lost.

The Road to Emmaus

Gathering dusk, dust
in puffs at our feet
as we walk, uncertain
of our directions down back ways,
talk in circles, pause, scuff
little graves in the road with our toes.
After a while we noticed someone walking
with us; we couldn't say why exactly,
but he seemed from far away.
Besides, he hadn't heard of the earthquake, or the death
of all our hopes. Our hushed
voices drifted among us
until we were only
drifting voices. When we stopped
to rest and eat in the warm light of an inn
he knelt with towel and water and began
to wash the dust from our feet. We stared
too surprised to speak.
He took the bread and broke it; then we knew
who leads us from the dark to come with him;
alone again but not alone, renewed,
we ate that broken bread, at one with him.

The Man Born Blind

John 9: 1-39

What we don't see is how a man
born blind, a beggar, suddenly is no more
blind than the rest of us. His story
about a wandering rabbi who rubbed mud
in his eyes seems, at the least, unlikely:
we don't see what good a poultice would have done,
or how the sins that stunted him in the womb
were suddenly all forgiven.
We don't see what made him this rabbi's business anyway,
or what kind of rabbi would heal on the Sabbath,
which is labor and defies the Law.
Now he is gone, following his "prophet";
though we were always nice to him, he left
with hard stares from his clear eyes
and bitter words:
we just don't see how he could call us blind.

Loaves and Fishes

Please stop asking me if I was thinking
symbolically. I was hungry,
that was all. The loaves and fishes
were my dinner, and enough
bread for a snack on the walk
back home. I'm always hungry,
ask my mother. But when I heard
my distant cousin Jesus speak his words
I forgot my body, forgot to eat or drink
as the sun turned red and the sea
shimmered like hammered copper.
I offered my little food to feed
the multitude of listeners,
and all were fed. A miracle? No.
Jesus spoke in the air we breathe,
stood on the land where we grow our bread,
behind him the sea teeming with fish.
Air, land, water are our world,
our life, and God
within them all
gave us this food, kept us sharing
to become one body
that will never hunger again.

The Road to Damascus

Arid light. Dust kicked up by donkeys' hooves
glitters as it falls, the long rutted road
unwinds into silence. Nothing moves
in the burning air; my breath and heart slowed
and flesh about to melt like candle wax
I cannot shield myself; even my bones
burn in this light, an angry voice attacks
my whole life as I lie utterly alone.
Soon soft hands and voices will come to soothe
my pain and heal the scabs that seal my eyes
and blind me with the darkness of my blood;
soon I will open my eyes, my voice, rise
and preach, heart open at last to the truth,
eyes open to the bright darkness of God.

St. Thomas

John 20:24-29

Nothing really matters but flesh and blood,
Then death, at worst my Teacher's death, his flayed
Flesh stretched out shuddering on blood-stained wood.

Where do our spirits go when we die? Could
Heaven be all around us if they stayed
With us like breaths caressing flesh and blood?

Why did Jesus choose to die in shame? Should
He not have used his nimble tongue and played
Fool against fool, and let that blood-stained wood

Hold up Barabbas' body to be food for crows? He could
Have lived, but chose to trade
His life for ours, give us his flesh and blood

At that last meal. Why? I wonder what good
That did, compared to this: his friends betrayed
To live in fear, minds' eyes fixed on blood-stained wood?

I asked all this and more, but then he stood
Alive among us, and my questions weighed
No more than breaths. I felt his flesh and blood,
And knew the answers left on blood-stained wood.

The Cup That I Drink

Mark 10:35-45

All the tables in Heaven are round
and all the places set
for someone you have never met on your right
and someone else on your left
who serves you first your bread
and then your wine
which you then serve to the person on your right
(counterclockwise because this is eternity)
and because when you lived by the hands of clocks
you thought there might not be enough
bread and wine and time
but there is always enough to pass on
until your hands are empty
because when your hands are empty they hold
everything that was ever yours.

Jordan

Chaff sweeps up in the desert wind like sand,
eddies, vanishes like the last hot breath
of day under the fire-red sun.
We stand clustered like sheaves of wheat still unthreshed,
heads bowed as angry words blaze over us,
scorch us like heat shimmering from the earth—
nowhere to flee, nothing to cover us.
Burning chaff, John shouts, is all we are worth.
But, winding just behind that rigorous voice,
the river flows to dissolve our sin,
wash away our chaff; we may rejoice
when we emerge, naked and finally clean.
Without this water we are empty hulls;
Once we are bathed within it, we are full.

Lady Day, March 25

Candle flames burn in blood
colored glass, unstirred
by breath or motion. Mary's face
looks neither to fire nor blood,
nowhere but the red-rimmed
dark where God
cell by cell enters his world, a curled life
pressing against the boundaries of her body as he
will reach the boundaries of pain
anyone can bear. In her, in him,
in him,
in birth, in death,
the year begins again, our lives
begin again.

Living Water

John 4:1-26

Seeping through walls of deep wells
or rising clean from deep springs
to still and take on
the colors of the sky
or fog mirrors until they clear
to take the shapes of faces
looking back through eyes
transparent as rain:
blood and breath of the earth
given to us, life
given to us in every cell
of our bodies, spirit
given to us so we need never thirst.

Rising

John 21: 1-14

Slow waking.
No light this far down,
dark of salt and stone,
cold water almost motionless,
only ripples, interlocking, rocking
in slow swells under boats and weather
far above
rising
until light wavers like a white face blurred by gauze,
broken by hulls' shadows still long
in the first white light after dawn,
long meshes of string and stones
paid out where he said to cast our nets
and the catch so heavy our boats creaked
with the strain and our arms could hardly
bend to haul that flailing mass over the rails until fish spilled
across the decks glittering
like a cache of silver coins
and he who had died stood before us
smiling, motioned us home to the shore
and a new world warming in the winds of spring, the sun
stronger every day, the fire he had built on the beach
flushing our faces as we stood together, each
silent before the silent man who had come home from death,
the fire subsiding to white ash, the wind a held breath

until we remembered to broil the fish, break bread;
we, the first drawn into the dark and cold with him and then
wakened with him, shared one last meal and rose, human again.

Easter Dawn

I.
The moon, past full, narrows like the white
of a closing eye; when the last
crescent sets a stone
rolls across the mouth of the tomb,
all doors shut.

II.
We wake to bells,
small bells' clatter and bronze hums
too low to hear with ear alone; we feel
clappers drop and mouths swing up,
shadows in their hollows like the earth's
shadow on the moon, swing down
still droning, echoing
the lowest voices, overlapping, smoothing,
rock to rest, the last strokes
no longer sound but wingbeats
pulsing in widening circles as the bells
go still, echoes sing
through the open door, the tomb
fills with light like a full moon
and eyes open to the world made new.

The Bronze Serpent

Hard susurrus
of scales on sand,
sinuous tracks we see too late.
Sharp whispers puncture
our bodies and we lie
too weak to stand, shivering
on the burning sand.

So many years of wandering
parched with thirst,
no paths out of scorched rock
and sand shifting
like the tracks of snakes.
Better to lie down and die,
look up with clouding eyes at the sky
grown dark except for the cross
Moses our prophet raised:
the bronze serpent
coiled around it shines
facet by facet, scale by scale:
white light breaks into rainbows
in our tearing eyes
as we look up, as we are drawn
up, the poison of our lives drawn
from our wounds
and cleansed to living water,

water that will flow
in lazy curves bright in the sun
when we reach our home,
water that will flow
from a broken body
raised into the sky
to guide us home to God.

Lazarus

John 11: 5-27

Four days I lay in dark perpetual night,
In death, that night in which we lie alone,
Our bodies sealed away from air and light,
Our bodies all our goods, our houses stone.

"You come in time, O Lord, to see us weep!
Where were you, Lord," far-off, faint voices cried,
"When Lazarus fell ill, and fell asleep?
You left a man who loved you, and he died."

Mary and Martha wept, and Jesus wept.
But then he said, "Your brother is not dead.
He is alive in me, though he has slept
Four days, and you believe his soul has fled."

"Then roll away the stone, and you will see
The resurrection and the life I give
To all who love me and believe in me;
Though they are dead and buried, they shall live."

I knew that I was not alone, that death
Like life is blessed, the grave a holy place;
I walked into the light and drew my breath,
Walked out of darkness toward the Lord's bright face,

Rejoined the holy life we live on earth
Where God is life within us all our days,
Where every moment is another birth,
Where every breath and living voice sings praise,

Sings praise to God who is our life, whose love
Transfigures us with gladness strong and deep,
Whose power pulls us to the light above,
Whose light will make us all arise from sleep.

Legion

> And the demons begged him, "If you cast us out, send us
> away into the herd of swine." And he said to them, "Go."
> So they came out and went into the swine; and behold, the
> whole herd rushed down the steep bank into the sea, and
> perished in the waters.—Matthew 8: 31-32

Rooted in the fleshy
pleasure of rubbing
dust and hardscrabble ground,
trotters clicking on the baked
black crust that yields
a few dry husks,
snouts sensitive as fingertips
brushing nubs of broken food.
Sows roll over
half asleep, sigh with milk building and the tugs
and warm flow into fumbling mouths
until
they stumble waking to their feet and know
they are pink and naked and so hungry.

Once awake,
what is there to do but die?

Jonah

Waters closed over me like the leaden cocoon of sleep.
I fled from God as far as I could when I was awake,
Fled from myself and found myself. That was my big mistake.
Every nightmare of my life opened its dark mouth; the deep
Teemed with monsters, blind searching teeth; I prayed
    to God to keep
Me sane, blind monster among blind monsters,
    cleanse my sin, break
My pride. Broken, stinking like spoiled meat, I labored to make
My peace with God: I preached and taught, played shepherd
    to his sheep.

And got no thanks from him, my only pay the shade of a tree
He killed off with a worm. My eyes streamed, my skin cracked,
    the cool
Shelter gone; then I knew: the blaring sun, the storm at sea,
The eyeless monsters, the worm, the tree, were only tools
In God's hands as he made his elaborate joke on me,
A monster in the dark and in the light of day a fool.

Who Shall Be First?

Luke 14:7-14

All the tables in Heaven are round
and every place the same, set
for someone you have never met on your right
and someone else on your left
who gives you first your bread
and then your wine
which you pass on to the person on your right
(counterclockwise because this is eternity)
holding back nothing and
holding onto nothing
because you are given nothing
except to take what you need
and pass the rest on, and because
when you have nothing
you have everything.

II. Put Your Hand on Compost

Envy

Fists clenched in frustration: flesh in hot folds, cold stabs
as fingernails bite the palms in crescents, mold cold stabs.

Open a fist. Palm smooth again, hand empty.
Curl it shut like a spider whose fangs hold cold stabs.

Remember, we used to be friends. Loosen your jaw, smile.
Show how your teeth lock together: some real, some gold, cold
    stabs.

Drop by drop, over lifetimes, stalactites sharpen
in the moonless dark, grow down, infinitely slowed cold stabs.

We lie together in the rigid dark. You clutch what should be mine.
I count what I still have: heartbeats, breaths. A clock tolls cold
    stabs.

The clock runs because its weights fall, too slowly to see.
Weighed down by emptiness inside we grow old, cold, stab.

Wrath

Hand of Glory: a thief's severed hand, used for crime, bursts fire
when lit like candles; melting fat smolders, low flames climb,
 burst fire.

So let's shake hands. The dead thief's hand works magic—
 opens doors.
So does yours, so plump, so manicured—the buffed nails shine,
 burst fire.

Doors close. I wipe my hand. Salamanders squirm
 on forest floors,
safe from searing heat though rotten wood around their slime
 bursts fire.

Wolves howl in the pleasure of blood indistinguishable from pain.
Red, heavy, the dim moon drags away from earth, climbs,
 bursts fire.

Hooked teeth glisten in icy light; your bared teeth,
 white as though clean,
glisten in your smile. My blood, behind our pantomime,
 bursts fire.

Put your hand on compost, feel the heat. But blood is hotter,
anger the shudder and hiss of flesh that will, in time, burst fire.

Avarice

I still keep money from my paper route, coins I would freeze,
    hold tight
in albums arranged by date and mint. Some coins get spent,
    these hold tight.

Silver crescents wink in change like slivers of the moon.
Piled too high they shift and slide; my fingers curl, seize,
    hold tight.

The world is paved with lost coins, dented bent and caked
    with dirt.
Head down, back bent, I fall as though in prayer to my knees,
    hold tight.

Real silver feels soapy, and takes a black mark from my teeth.
    Copper tastes
like blood. Blood heat smooths hard edges as I squeeze,
    hold tight.

I lie all night, rigid in my blood, count everything I own:
never enough! and all falling from my hands. I pray: *please,
    hold tight.*

Never enough! I cannot hold enough, and what I lose rolls free,
grows cold. I too grow cold, locked in a grip that nothing frees,
    hold tight.

Sloth

Something happened somewhere, not to me. The mills of God
    grind slow,
the saying goes; I seem to wear a millstone as the daily plod
    grinds slow.

In by nine, out at five precisely. Snug soundproof cubicle
in earth tones, piped-in birdsongs. Growth in this artificial sod
    grinds slow.

Sloths hang from jungle branches, backs curved like
    waxing moons.
Molars slide over slimy leaves. Winds in humid air, hot as blood,
    grind slow.

How many toes do sloths have? I guess I could look it up.
They snuffle upside-down; their steps, two-toed or three-toed,
    grind slow.

Sloths' toenails, two or three, click as they walk. My world
    is quieter.
Co-workers pass my cubicle; we all, well-clothed, well-shod,
    grind slow.

Home in my snug apartment, TGIF and all, TV on.
Free to do nothing, nothing to do. Nothing, O God, grinds slow.

Gluttony

Dinner: knife and fork like sword and spear I attack, open wide
to get it all in during the news, sit back jaw slack, open wide.

Steamed baked roasted broiled, best of all fried, hot cold
    just warm,
solid liquid or crackling in fat—jaw slack I sit back, open wide.

In heaven the clouds are whipped cream, mountains cheese;
fish swim in lemon butter; birds fly crackling on roasting racks,
    opened wide.

In heaven the buildings are restaurants where you never have
    to tip;
they're plastered with fudge, shingled with pancakes in thick
    stacks. Open wide!

But here on earth blood thuds sluggishly through a belly bloated
like a full moon. Still the hungry mouth, teeth scummed with
    plaque, opens wide.

Fat hangs in slabs, pendulums of flesh. At one end the mouth
opens, chews; at the other end of tubes and juices, the black crack
    opens wide.

Lechery

Joke: a woman got a checkup. The doctor said, "Open wide."
"You mean my mouth?" We laugh and repeat, nodding our heads,
   "Open wide."

Petite tall slender plump, olive brunette or best of all blonde
(real blonde at the cunt), breasts and ass jiggling as they wriggle
   in bed, open wide.

In heaven the women are all Playmates of the Month:
firm nipples and clits, soft everything else, skin sleek, lips red,
   open wide.

In heaven the women never say a word (*yes* is understood);
they jiggle and wriggle, smile and flirt and lie back instead,
   open wide.

But here on earth blood thuds as belly slides on belly slick
   with sweat.
Rotten-fish smell. A sewer of blood pours out of the moon,
   dead, open wide.

Teeth line that bloody mouth, curved in to stick and swallow
   like a snake.
Men fall back cold, drained white except where their wounds
   bled, open wide.

Pride

> The world's longest fingernails are those of Shridhar Chil-
> lal (India), who last cut his fingernails in 1952. On July 8,
> 1998 the nails on his left hand had a total length of 20 ft
> 2.25 in (6.15 m).—*Guinness World Records 2002*

I have no need for jewelry or fine clothes; I am, instead,
   growing beauty
lambent like mother-of-pearl cupping new pearls in an
   oyster bed, growing beauty.

When I was a child my teeth wore them down to nothing but nubs.
Then beauty came with pain: as they grew out scar tissue bled,
   growing beauty.

They began as crescents thin as the moon pared almost dark,
then pure white flowed in streams from the quick's dull red,
   growing beauty.

I have given them my body: legs that rarely walk anymore,
arms that ache to keep them raised, hands that cannot
   hold bread, growing beauty.

Beauty, the sternest of masters, holds me to my task
and though my body shrivels my soul is fed, growing beauty.

Long as swords, curved like cobras' hoods, they have taken my life
and given it back as art: now I inspire wonder and dread,
   growing beauty.

III. Via Crucis: The Way of the Cross

Corpus Christi

Anonymous
amorphous
crowds pushed back
to clear a path for a dying man
whipped raw, welts welling red, face
a scarlet mask.
Shuffles and murmurs, no words
for his pain, for the whips
burning our backs too, for this dust and blood
and smell of death. Still,
we follow. When the soldiers
close behind him, we
follow him holding the crosses
of all our lives, follow him
who is all of us
up the hill, for centuries.

At the top of the hill
we too will have faces

I. Pilate

Discs of marble in a white face
untouched by the sun, white
toga too crisp to hang like cloth.
If I shook my head
hard enough, red drops would sully it. I stand
still, hot in my blood, hard hands
holding me up, watch his white hands
squirm like nervous animals, watch
water glisten as it breaks
into drops still clean, still cool,
drink every drop with my eyes.

II. The Cross

Raw wood, rough carpentry. My shoulder sags
to accept the load once more: door-beam, roof-beam, fencepost,
all the same. You let your back
bend, let the weight lean into you, reach
around and pull the beam down to balance it, stagger
a little if you must for balance, then walk, the weight
now yours. Up the hill. Try to step
in time with the soldiers. Ignore how your ear
sticks to the wood with blood. Try to see
where in the bright dust your next step
will fall, try to pull up

III. First Fall

Liquid snap at my ankle as the plank
I was carrying slapped the ground.
Dust too sour to breathe. Please
don't help me up. Father,
I will learn to carry it right. I promise
never to let it fall again.

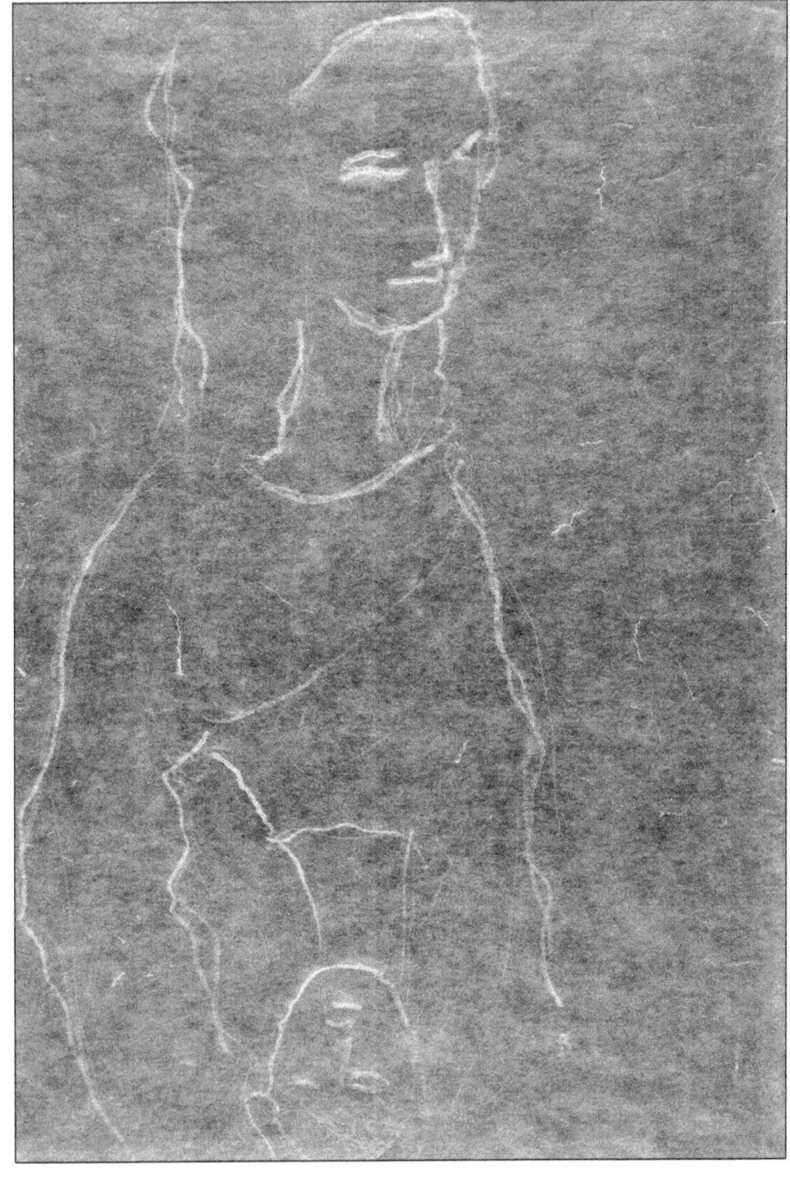

IV. Mary

Mother, you lift me
halfway, your hand
cradles my head as it lolls back
to sleep. Stronger
hands pull me up, pull
you away. Your face,
unveiled, has grown old.
Mother, what
has become of your son?

V. Simon of Cyrene

My face glowing white in a crown
of iron wavers above me, blocking out the sun.
Hands sling me upright like a sack of wheat.
Beardless, hard, black open mouth, my face bellows
words thick like spittle. My face on a man
hands seize, shove
under the cross. His shoulder sags, he lets
the weight lean into him, he
shrugs, hooks
his arm on the cross-beam, pulls down, staggers
a little for balance and walks, the weight
now his. He walks like a man who knows the march
uphill
will never end.

VI. Veronica

Cool hands, wavering
woman's form. Thin linen
molds to my face, blood and sweat
blinding, salt. They strip off the cloth, I see
a woman's face sealed shut with tears:
unveiled the face of a stranger, naked
a sister.

VII. Second Fall

Burning full length on these stones, back
bent like a broken snake.
Red spatters like dropped coins run into lines
on a paving stone, every thorn a pen point
drawing my face in blood.
I can raise only my head, but hands
will haul me up again, boots
kick my face into dust.

VIII. The Women of Jerusalem

Blurred shapes "like trees walking" that blind man said
after I spit on his eyes. Blurs
nod, bow. Which
shaded my face with palm leaves? They bend
like trees under wind, but the dust
lies still, spotted with blood. Which
pulled on my arm to hold me back when I struck
the Temple thieves? Which
stroked my hair out in the hot street,
under her black dress shadows rich with blood?

IX. Third Fall

This time I will not get up. I will never
stand on my feet again. They will carry me
the last few steps of the way, a body
already shouldered for its funeral march.
Blank-eyed soldiers stare down at me,
lances' butts at their heels, points
burning like stars in the noon sky.
They are about to kill me. If I could
raise my arms, I would embrace them all.

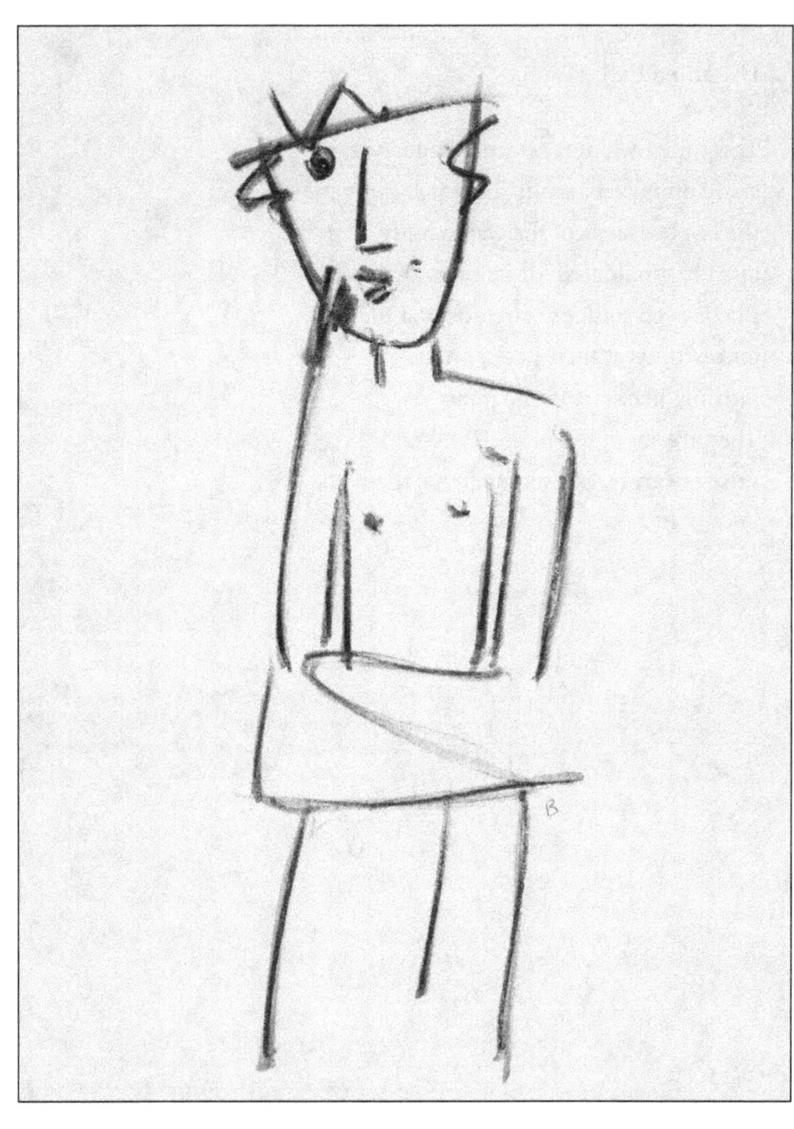

X. Naked

They stripped off my tunic without touching me,
shucked off my sandals like dead skin.
The flat of a blade slides up my leg
stiff as a striking snake. The last cloth
covering me falls away. I cover
my shriveled member with my hands, the soldier
laughs as he sheaths his sword.

Nothing any more is mine.

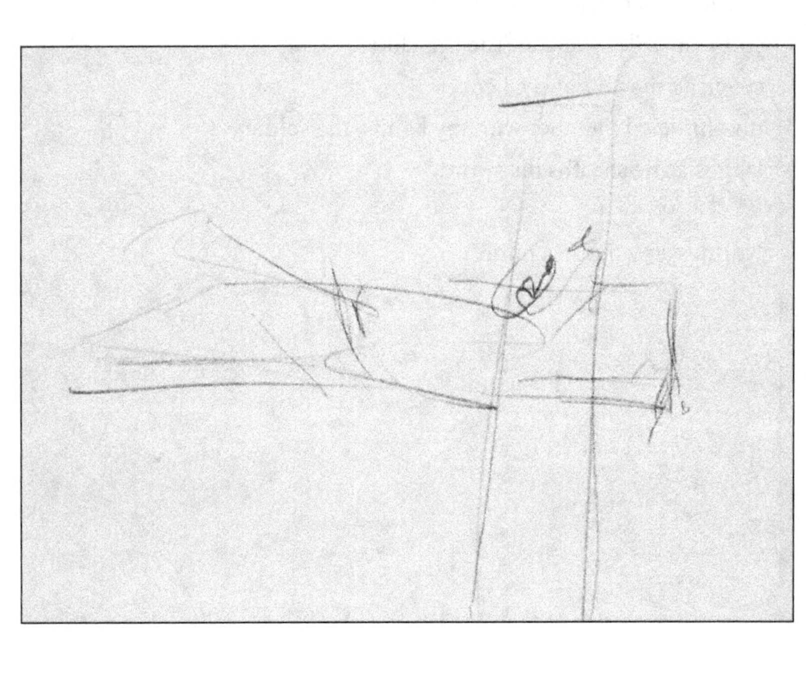

XI. Nailed to the Cross

Iron rings on iron, echoed by screams.
Next they will come for me.
Muffled thumps of wood on wood. You swing
the mallet with both hands, let the shock
run down your body into the ground. Your hands
ache, curl shut, but they straighten
your fingers, one by one, hold them
almost tenderly. A hammer swings up, drops.

Who is screaming?

When will he stop?

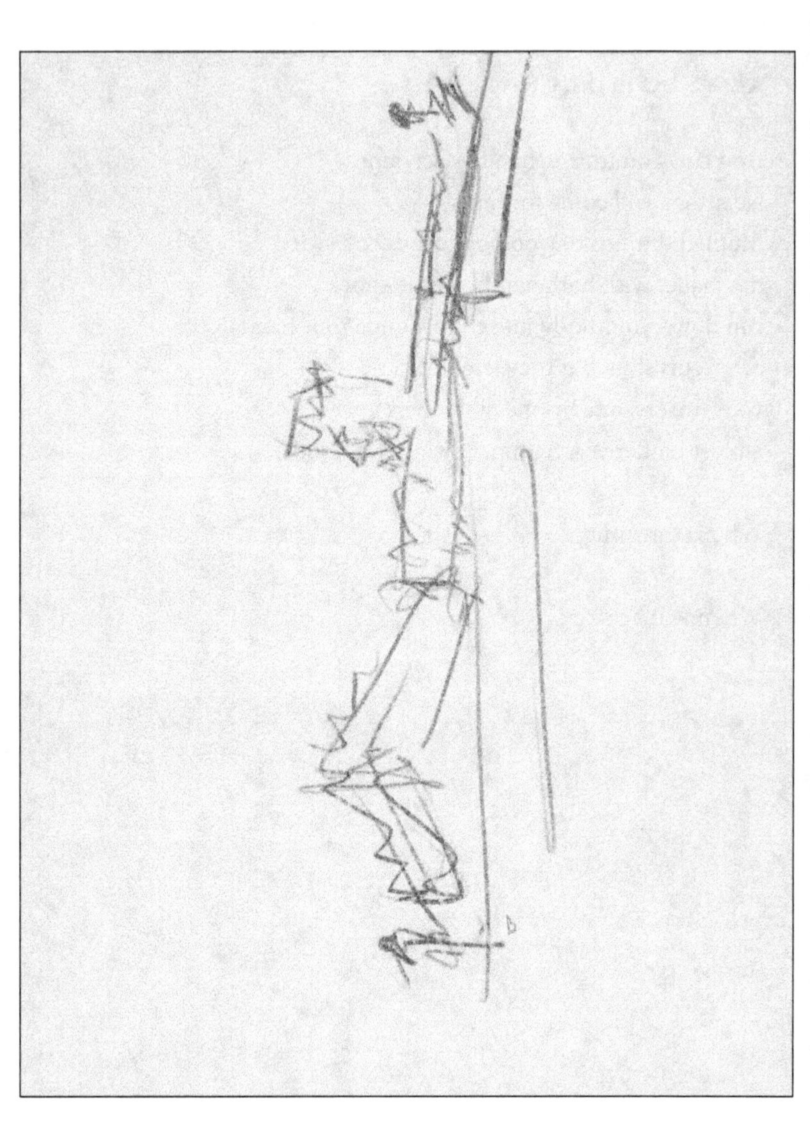

XII. Crucified

Raised a few feet over a low hill
I can see to the edge of the world.
A boy in Galilee struggles to please his father
and turns embarrassed from his mother's love,
a man in a garden calls to his father and hears only
silence broken by marching boots
come to carry him up this hill, silence
he filled with words even here
where the world is too wide and the wind too strong
for words to carry, breath to fill
lungs heavy with blood, this body
slipping down, scraping its raw back
on raw wood, shivering in the sun. Mother,
don't worry. There is no more pain. Father,
forgive me. I didn't understand your silence.

XIII. Dead

There is nothing more they can do to this body.
Breath still, heart stopped, blood dry, it lies
empty. Fingertips knead the torn flesh whole.
Crisp water, cloth.
Cloying aloe, oil of myrrh.
Hands I know so well
caress the long flanks, place the spread arms
at my sides like closing wings, a voice
I know so well hushes me once more
to rest as a bird folds into sleep at dusk.

XIV. Buried

and the first cool air flows over the body
raised on bent backs hurrying to bury it
before the sun sets.
      Hands linger a moment,
smooth the shroud. The stone rasps shut.

Linen molds to the body's face, no breath to lift it,
settles along the flesh grown cold and stiff. If the cloth
rustles I cannot hear it
here, still and dark as before the world was made.
      This is strange.
There should not be stars inside stone.

It is finished.

About the Editor

Deborah Fleming, former editor and director of the Ashland Poetry Press, is author of *Resurrection of the Wild: Meditations on Ohio's Natural Landscape* (2019), winner of the PEN-America Foundation's Diamonstein-Spielvogel Art of the Essay Award for 2020. She is also author of three collections of poems, *Morning, Winter Solstice* (2012), *Into a New Country* (2016), and *Earthrise* (2021); two chapbooks, *Migrations* (2005) and *Source of the River* (2018); and a novel, *Without Leave* (2014), winner of the Asheville Award. She has also published *"A man who does not exist": The Irish Peasant in W. B. Yeats and J. M. Synge* (1995) and *Towers of Myth and Stone: Yeats's Influence on Robinson Jeffers* (2015) and edited two collections of scholarly essays, *Learning the Trade: W. B. Yeats and Contemporary Poetry* (1992) and *W. B. Yeats and Postcolonialism* (2000). Winner of a Vandewater Poetry Award and grants from the National Endowment for the Humanities and National Council of Learned Societies, she has had three poems nominated for the Pushcart Prize.

www.ingramcontent.com/pod-product-compliance
Lightning Source LLC
Chambersburg PA
CBHW070737030726
47601CB00001B/47